**an
introduction
to...**

Using Newspapers and Periodicals

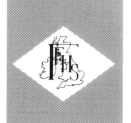

Colin R. Chapman

Federation of Family History Societies

Published by the
Federation of Family History Societies
The Benson Room, Birmingham and Midland Institute, Margaret
Street, Birmingham B3 3BS, England

Copyright © Colin R. Chapman 1993

ISBN 1-872094-70-8

Printed by Oxuniprint, Walton Street, Oxford OX2 2DP

The Federation of Family History Societies is a Registered Charity, No. 284520

CONTENTS

PREFACE

William Caxton introduced his novel printing press to England in 1477, the concept of movable type having been invented in 1455. This enabled, for the first time, multiple copies of a book or pamphlet or sheet to be produced without the laborious efforts by clerks and scriveners preparing handwritten copies. In 1500 Wynkyn de Warde, a former assistant of Caxton, set up his own printing business 'at the Sign of the Sun' beside St Bride's Church, off Fleet Street in London. Fleet Street was a major artery linking the City of London and St Paul's with Parliament and Westminster. Other printers and booksellers joined the secular and ecclesiastical lawyers, and their clerks and scriveners, whose businesses between Doctors' Commons and the Inns of Court drew them naturally to the area. Just over 200 years later, and just over 200 yards away, the initial issue of the *Daily Courant*, Britain's first regular daily newspaper was printed, so beginning an association that will forever be remembered between newspapers, periodicals and Fleet Street. Many British national dailies are no longer printed in that part of London, difficulties in transporting huge quantities of paper in and finished newsprint out, and new requirements for changing technologies encouraged proprietors away from that congested area, but it will be a long time before Fleet Street and newspapers cease to be used as synonyms, both internationally and in Britain.

In the following pages we shall discuss how newspapers and periodicals, those that rolled off the Fleet Street presses, and those published elsewhere, can be used to provide information, both essential and complementary, when compiling a local, social or family history.

Colin R. Chapman

THE GROWTH OF NEWSPAPERS AND PERIODICALS

Even if Ruskin described Fleet Street and the surrounding area as 'so many square leagues of dirtily printed falsehoods', the newspapers published there and elsewhere throughout the country offer some rich material for genealogists and family historians. The year 1702 may have marked the founding of the first regular daily paper, but for 200 years there had been a procession of newsbooks, news sheets, pamphlets and periodicals printed in Britain carrying news and articles of varying quality. Before leaping into some newspapers and periodicals, it is useful to remind ourselves how they have been produced. For us to appreciate fully what we are reading we should understand a little of how the 'news' has been collected and edited over the years, and who and what influenced these processes. Besides giving us a better background to the Fourth Estate, as the newspaper medium has been called (it has even been described as the Dangerous Estate, see Bibliography), a brief look at the history of British newspapers will enable us to interpret a published page better, and to realise that just because it is in print does not mean that it must be factual. Indeed, we shall see that to print stories in preference to facts was a legitimate way of avoiding the newspaper tax (Stamp Duty) of the eighteenth century; perhaps some reporters, editors and proprietors today have not yet appreciated that to print the truth no longer incurs a financial penalty.

The emergence of British newspapers and periodicals resulted from two needs: firstly the need for news of current or recent affairs; gentlemen in the country areas such as Members of Parliament back in their constituencies, wanting to know what the government (both Church and Crown) was up to in London that might affect the way of life for their families, servants and tenants; and merchants and traders wanting to know market prices for corn and other commodities, possibly affected by weather and internal travelling conditions, and with the growth of overseas trade from the mid-16th Century wanting details on ports and sailing vessels and assurance on the political stability of potential trading partners in Continental Europe and elsewhere. Secondly the need for literary entertainment brought about by the decline in travelling troupes of performers and the growth of the theatre in which written plays were performed, accelerated by the endowment of many schools, by merchants and gentlemen from the late 15th century, developing literacy and education in general.

Although the needs were there, and the technology introduced by Caxton in the latter half of the 15th Century was available in Britain, neither Church nor Crown was very stable in the 16th and 17th Centuries. The Reformation and then the Civil War made everyone suspicious of everyone else and those in power dared not trust their neighbours or subordinates and were unsure how long they were likely to remain in power. Meetings of ecclesiastical and secular potential trouble-makers were forbidden and the 'Establishment' attempted to protect itself and its interests by restricting the freedom of everybody. The 'Press' was among those subjected to restrictions or requiring expensive licences, if not being totally banned. Newsbooks, corantos and news sheets came and went as proprietors attempted to cope with or circumvent the legislation.

The first British newsbooks were in a pamphlet style modelled on Dutch corantos and emerged in relatively large numbers in the 1620s. A Star Chamber decree banned all newsbooks between 1632 and 1638, but on the eve of the Civil War there were many events which catalysed masses of publications, many illegal, with comment on the political situation. It has been calculated that over 1000 separate issues of different papers were published between 1620 and 1642. There were a dozen weekly newsbooks in London in 1644, eight of which were still being published in the early 1650s. During the Civil War many continental corantos or Intelligencers were published as English editions in London and the original pamphlet-style gave way to a single-leaf layout; those that were published daily were termed Diurnals. But Oliver Cromwell became equally worried that democracy in the shape of total freedom of the press was perhaps taking things a bit too far. Accordingly he tightened up existing Acts and Decrees, and in 1655 he appointed a Government Censor, effectively causing a state monopoly of news.

Immediately following the Restoration of the Monarchy in 1660, the Royalists were no better; although they abolished the post of Censor, the 1662 Printing Act created a Licenser, initially until 1679 and then revived from 1685 until 1695, which in effect perpetuated the censorship and monopoly of news. The *Oxford Gazette*, a weekly paper, was licensed in 1665, re-licensed as the *London Gazette* when it moved to London in 1666 and as such has continued to this day as Britain's oldest surviving newspaper, albeit weekly. But during the six years between 1679 and 1685 when no licences were strictly needed, several Royal proclamations curbed the press and issued constant reminders of the laws of seditious libel. However, in 1695 restrictions were lifted and papers sprung up like mushrooms, appearing weekly, twice and thrice weekly, and then on 11 March 1702 the *Daily Courant* was born, which incidently was printed at Ludgate Circus at the bottom of Fleet Street. Britain's first evening paper, the *Evening Post*, was established soon after, in 1705, with the *Dublin Evening Post* coming on the scene in 1719. Outside London, provincial newspapers were not far behind; for example the *Worcester Post Man* in 1695 (becoming *Berrow's Worcester Journal*, and still in publication) and the *Norwich Post* in 1701 (becoming the *Gazette*). These papers generally selling for 1d carried mostly foreign or national news; and as there were no reporters as such, papers openly copied each other's texts. Proprietors soon realised that their publishing costs could be recovered not only from direct sales, but by carrying advertisements, initially of post-coach and carriers' timetables or for missing persons or arriving vessels. In the early days, however, most advertisements were mild and factual; outlandish and sensational claims about a product came much later.

Today's claims and counter-claims to be the oldest surviving provincial newspaper will rumble on forever. The *Worcester Journal* and the *Stamford Mercury* both claim to have originated first, while the *Northampton Mercury*, established in 1720, claims to have the earliest origins with a continuous run to the present; unlike others it continued publication throughout the 1926 General Strike. There is a chronological table of provincial newspapers in Wiles' *Freshest Advice* (see Bibliography).

The explosion of the free press was instantly of great concern to the politicians but they recognized that reintroducing censorship would be unpalatable. The press would have to be muzzled by other means. Thus in 1712 a Stamp Act (10 Anne c.18) was introduced, imposing a tax of 1d on a full news sheet and ½d on a half sheet for every copy of a paper, and a duty of 1s. per advertisement per issue. It was with some justification the opponents to this duty called it a 'tax on knowledge'. Pamphlets were also taxed, but at only 2s. per sheet per issue, regardless of how many copies were published. Several papers increased their selling prices to 1½d and increased their advertising rates; but sales dropped dramatically and many provincial papers were forced to close: the government breathed a sigh of relief.

As with all legislation, the determined found ways of using the statute to their advantage: the 1d tax per issue for a full sheet was the maximum imposed, and so two sheets still only attracted a 1d duty. In addition an extended paper could be made to resemble a pamphlet and be registered as such, so attracting less duty. And so some previously one-sheet twice-weekly newspapers such as the *Flying Post*, in London and the provinces, became cheaper multiple-sheet weeklies. In any case, reports coming in were not always up-to-date, having to rely on messengers, pigeons and semaphore. It made little difference in those days if news was two or three or more days old, in fact it makes little difference today; we have become obsessed by the spontaneity of instant electronic communications and one proprietor wanting a 'scoop' in advance of others. With open plagiarism in the past, such immediacy was unnecessary, and so were ulcers and heart attacks caused by the pressures of urgency. In fact with less pressure the weeklies were generally more accurate, better laid out and altogether superior publications.

Many proprietors, particularly smaller printers, solved the Stamp Duty problem much more simply, they ignored it and sold their unstamped illegal papers at ½d each through street vendors. Others with ingenuity disguised the news by portraying it as stories, poems and articles which, when published, were exempt from the Duty. Thus the concept of comment, rather than pure fact was born which, as cynically mentioned above, has continued to today, even though news as such is no longer taxed.

The larger papers, paying the Duty, were so incensed by the activities of their smaller enterprising rivals that they supported the government's introduction of the 1725 Stamp Act (11 Geo I c.8) which brought all newspapers, irrespective of length, under the requirements of the 1712 Act. Although some extended London papers reduced their sizes to half sheets of four pages, none went out of business, whereas in the provinces the Act successfully achieved the government's aim to force several papers to close. In fact in the 1730s there were six dailies and nine in the 1770s, including the *London Daily Post*, *Public Advertiser* and *Daily Advertiser*, the latter titles indicating their major source of income. The 1725 Act, however, was treated by some thirty London entrepreneurs with the same contempt as the 1712 legislation; they continued to publish and sell their unstamped papers through street vendors. The *Gentleman's Magazine*, more of a periodical than a newspaper, was founded in 1731; detail on this publication is given below. In 1743, however, legislation (16 Geo II c.2) against the vendors, followed by a few prosecutions, reported with glee and at length in the legal press, totally killed off for ever this section of the 'free' press.

Returning to the attack with confidence in 1757 the government added another ½d per copy and doubled the advertisement duty to 2s., and in 1776 yet another ½d causing most papers to be sold at 3d or more each. In London the daily papers attempted to respond by increasing paper sizes and squeezing in more text by changing from three- to four-column formats; some became Chronicles with eight smaller pages, but the weeklies in general went out of business whilst the provincial weeklies enjoyed increased sales, mainly from the gentry returning home from London to their country seats. Naturally there were occasions, as today, when spectacular news such as the Jacobite Rebellion and the American Revolution boosted sales. Even so, several weekly newspapers resorted to pamphlets again with articles, poetry and critiques, and when made available for Sunday reading, set the style now traditional for our present Sunday papers. But the London papers could not originally get their papers to the counties to be able to compete with the flourishing provincial press. From 1784 the situation changed with the introduction of mail coaches by John Palmer. Roads were improving anyway and although postal charges between towns was considerable, Members of Parliament, and somehow their clerks, enjoyed concessionary rates.

Newspaper proprietors were not slow in learning of this and began courting MPs, so successfully that some actually became shareholders in papers, while others were suitably rewarded for their assistance. A Post Office survey in 1782 showed that 3,070,000 London papers were sent to the provinces and 60,000 within London; and in one week in 1789 MPs sent out 63,177 papers, compared with only 12,909 being sent legitimately by the Post Office clerks. Becoming rather concerned that too many of the working classes were beginning to take an interest in current affairs, in 1789 the government increased the Stamp Duty from 1½d to 2d and banned the hiring of newspapers (it was well known that coffee houses, inns and taverns bought newspapers to attract increasingly literate customers) and thus readership totals were well above sales figures; in some places up to 80 people read one paper. But this move merely helped the papers to increase their sales. In fact in 1787 the Post Office had already set up a separate department to deal with newspapers and in 1792 the 'System' had to give in to current practices and permitted papers to be distributed free of charge; in addition, franking of papers was dropped, mainly because so many frankings were forged. But in 1798 another attempt to curb the papers was made by increasing the Stamp Duty yet again, this time to 2½d per copy.

Printing technology improved with the invention in 1800 of the iron-framed Stanhope Press giving good quality papers but at only 250 copies per hour until 1814 when Koenig's steam press enabled

1000 copies per hour to be printed. *The Times* was the first to install the new inventions, but others followed over the next 15 years, the *Manchester Guardian* and the *Staffordshire Advertiser* in 1828, the *Western Times* in 1835 and the *Leeds Intelligencer* in 1836. But the government was still determined to exercise some control; it had laready increased the Stamp Duty from 2½d to 3d in 1804, but in 1815 made a desperate attack, increasing the advertisement duty to 3s.6d and the Stamp Duty to 4d. However, industrialisation and enterprise could not be stopped. The development and expansion of the railways from 1830 and the setting up of an independent carrier service in 1840, by Mr. W.H. Smith, based near to Fleet Street, together provided an excellent distribution network. The introduction of the electric telegraph also from 1840 enabled reports to be quickly transmitted from agents to the publishing unit, rather than relying on the pigeons and semaphore mentioned above.

With so many opportunities for producing and distributing papers to a rapidly increasing population with improving literacy, individual proprietors had little chance to establish or expand newspaper businesses. Thus syndicates emerged capable of raising the capital but several, such as the Chartist, soon failed as committee management was far more indecisive than a single owner, such as of the *Poor Man's Guardian* or the strong editors of *The Times*, two John Walters (father and son) and Thomas Barnes. The provincial papers tended to be owned, and in many cases edited, by local businessmen and tradesmen intent on promoting their businesses. Thus these papers had been politically neutral, deliberately so, to appeal to both parties. But as the Napoleonic Wars dragged on they took on a radical role and in some areas new papers were established specifically to promote an ideal: the *Leicester Journal* was established in 1810 to oppose the Tory council, whereas the Westmorland Gazette was founded in 1818 by Tories. But readers began to lose interest in reading about politics and from 1830 a plethora of 'useful knowledge' papers and periodicals were established, increasing their sales with every issue; several of the established papers reduced the length of their parliamentary reports and included sensational news and more murders, police cases and violence to increase their sales. The colourless fiction of the *Penny Magazine* was equally unattractive to readers and lead to its collapse in 1846.

In parallel with technological developments and improving literacy, the government decided after the Napoleonic Wars that press regulation was no longer necessary. Accordingly the heavy taxes and Stamp and Excise Duties on newspapers and their advertisements, which had been imposed specifically to control them by licensing and closure, were gradually withdrawn from 1830. The Duty imposed on pamphlets was removed in 1833, and that on almanacs in 1834. Advertisement Duty was reduced from 3s.6d to 1s.6d in 1833 and abolished altogether in 1853. In 1836 Newspaper Stamp Duty was reduced from 4d to 1d and in 1855 that was also abolished. Excise Duty on paper was reduced in 1836 from 3d to 1½d per pound and withdrawn in 1861. The prices of papers fell from 6d or more to 2d, and in some cases to ½d each. Newspapers could now be a viable enterprise on their own, rather than a hobby or sideline for a bookseller or printer. From the mid-1850s advertisements appeared in every paper, and new papers sprung up everywhere, building on the traditional chapbooks, broadsheets and street ballads. Whereas there had been 76 newspapers and periodicals published in England and Wales in 1781, by 1851 there were 563 newspapers alone, and the numbers leaped even higher in 1854, 1856 and 1862 as Duties were successively abolished. The papers, now free from their shackles, could respond entirely to their readers' needs, rather than be constantly conscious of a regulatory government. The Press Association was formed in 1868 to collect and disseminate telegraphic reports quickly to all Fleet Street based papers. Many provincial papers appointed agents or opened their own offices nearby to collect information for their readers. Reports, advertisements and notices that you find in newspapers and periodicals, particularly from this time, are packed with useful information on individuals and localities.

THE CONTENT OF NEWSPAPERS AND PERIODICALS

We have to accept that newspaper proprietors were, and are, in business to make money. They are not usually philanthropists, although some may have subsequently been philanthropic. They know that their readers will, as they always have, buy a paper or a periodical for the quality of its news, its entertainment or its advertisements. Thus proprietors mould the content and style of their publications to appeal to their readership; even medium-sized towns could support more than one local paper catering for different tastes.

As mentioned above, both local (provincial) and national (in the past, London-based) newspapers originally contained only national and international news, and often in very vague terms, probably because the reports the papers themselves received were vague; regular or accurate reports from 'correspondents' were not introduced until the 1820s, initially by *The Times*. It was also true that country gentlemen, or at least their wives, knew the local news anyway, and so had no requirement to read about that; they needed news on policies and strategies from London or the Continent. For these reasons, names of individuals, unless of eminent personalities or others experiencing exceptional circumstances, are unlikely to appear in early newspaper columns. In many cases, however, the accounts do provide some background information for a specific locality or particular time period and so are worth reading.

Local newspapers, as the 18th century progressed, began to include reports on more localised items, although a major national calamity or celebration, such as the death of the King or signing a Peace Treaty or a Coronation, tended to squeeze out local events, a pattern which continued into the present century. My great grandfather died at the same time as Edward VII and his death (my ancestor's, not the King's) and all others in Northampton at that time, were unreported. Conversely when news was thin, many papers carried quite inconsequential articles on events and people. Typical was an item such as the son (named and giving his age and physical description) of a local squire (named and giving his address) having just (the date) completed private tuition (naming his tutor), was about to enter a school (identified by name, location and the name of the headmaster). Whilst this may have been trivia to most readers, if any people in articles such as this are your ancestors, the information may be gold dust for you.

It is important to realise that even when a newspaper bore the name of a town or county or region it did not restrict its news to details on individuals or events from only within that area. The *Northampton Mercury*, for example, was the only paper published in that part of the country for many years and regularly reported events in Bedfordshire, Huntingdonshire, Cambridgeshire, Oxfordshire, Leicestershire and Rutland, as well as further afield. Accounts of local events invariably contain names of individuals, possibly your ancestors, doing all sorts of things: singing in the Methodist choral festival, acting in the pageant on the village green, getting lost on a Sunday School treat, winning prizes at local fetes or fairs for being the fastest swimmer or the strongest apprentice, growing the longest carrot or baking the tastiest cake or brewing the best elderflower wine; suing neighbours, giving evidence, acting as witnesses or being fined, or acting as the Magistrate or Constable in a variety of courts, buying or selling property, taking over the tenancy of an inn, participating in sports or passing examinations. Unusual weather conditions and scientific experiments, perhaps performed by an ancestor of yours, were often reported in the press. A group of children, all named, for whom a parish collection had been taken to enable them to be apprenticed to masters, whose names and trades were quoted, appeared in even a London paper, the *Post Boy* for 8 December 1720.

Although political commentary was common, reports of parliamentary proceedings were not permitted until 1771, and reporters were not officially allowed into the House until 1803. However, politicians, Whigs and Tories alike, quite openly and frequently, bribed newspaper owners to champion their causes. When in the early 18th century opposition MPs used the *London Evening Post* to promote their policies, government minsters responded by using public money to fund the *True Briton* and used government employees to write the articles; Walpole used £50,000 of Treasury funds to convince the opposition's *Morning Post* to support him. In the 19th Century the editor of *The Times* was said to the closer to the Prime Minister than the members of the Cabinet. All political articles should, therefore, be read with caution. Nothing changes!

After the introduction of the New Poor Laws from 1834, reports of Boards of Guardians are often very detailed providing intimate information on particular paupers. The local provisions for schooling adults and children attracted several column-inches. From the middle of the 19th Century, illustrations, drawings and sketches, and later on photographs, were incorporated into reports, perhaps with pictures of your family and their homes. Deliberations at Vestry Meetings, and later at Council Meetings, were often very colourful and reported with similar enthusiasm and comment, revealing the political persuasion of the proprietor or editor, rather than the decisions of councillors. If you have not yet used newspapers or periodicals in your historical research, you can get a flavour of the range of reports from 1750 to 1850 in Morsley's *News from the English Countryside* and for a similar time-period, Ashton's *Old Times* and his *Dawn of the 19th Century* (see Bibliography).

Most national and local newspapers contain formal notices or announcements of betrothals or engagements or weddings about to take place; from the early 1700s until the First World War, there was often an account of the 'fortune' or 'portion' that would accompany the bride, her dowry. Death announcements were similarly included as the 18th Century progressed, appearing next to the proposed marriages. In the early days, however, births did not appear as formal notices but often as idle commentary in the social columns. When formal announcements of birth did become popular in many papers, it was well into the 19th Century and they were then printed with the engagements, marriages and deaths. By this time newspaper proprietors saw these announcements almost as advertisements and charged accordingly for every such insertion. Thus those of humble means are unlikely to appear in such announcements or notices. A birth announcement was likely to mention both parents and the maiden name of the mother and often stated exactly where and when the child was born, and included a notice of the forthcoming Christening ceremony or baptism and named the intended godparents or sponsors, a useful finding aid for you if you are experiencing difficulty in tracing a baptismal entry.

In addition to formal notices of marriages and deaths there were extensive reports of weddings, with illustrations, and of obituaries and funerals. In the matrimonial reports until the Second World War, those who attended a wedding, the guests, as well as the best man, the bride's parents, bridesmaids, pageboys, ushers, and even the organist, the bellringers and who gave what present were all named in the reports with a note of where the couple went for their honeymoon. Today you will be lucky if you get the correct name of the couple under a photograph dominated by the name of the photographer; not much use for our descendants!

Obituary notices (obits), normally only of local or national personalities, but when news was thin, stretching further down the social spectrum, were really potted biographies of the deceased; these obits may include details on a spouse or former spouse or spouses and the political, religious and social groups with which the deceased was associated, just the sort of information that every family historian longs to discover, perhaps providing a lead into another series of records. Many reports on funerals, to this day in rural areas, state the names of the mourners and their relationship to the deceased, often vital genealogical data not available anywhere else; but sometimes misreported and names occasionally misspelled if the reporter or typesetter or proof-reader was tired or pushed for time. Some funerals were reported at length, stating the time of departure of the cortege from a named address, a description of the funeral carriage and even the horses drawing it and their owners, the route it took, when it arrived at the church or cemetery, the names of the pall bearers, and if committed to a family vault who was already interred these, who conducted the service and who were the undertakers and who sent wreaths. Some funeral reports even include biographical details on the deceased, and possibly unpleasant details on the cause of death, information that one would normally expect to find in (or hope was omitted from) an obituary notice. A few weeks later, and after probate had been granted, if the deceased was a local or national worthy the value of the estate might be reported locally or nationally; in some cases a fuller account was printed in the newspaper of the main provisions and conditions in the will.

During times of war, both national and local newspapers have published names of those killed or missing, and of local heroes or those civilians and members of the armed forces awarded medals or decorations for gallantry or bravery. Victims of fighting and accidents, people falling in rivers and off hay waggons, being burned in barns and houses, being assailed by attackers and being run over by horses and carriages, are likely to be named in newspaper reports. Some London newspapers provided a daily *Court Circular* or diary of what senior members of the Royal Family or nobility or Government Ministers will be doing today and what they did yesterday; some local newspapers offered similar information on the local gentry.

In maritime areas the times of high and low tides, the arrivals and departures of ferries, sailing, steam and other vessels, crucial for the welfare of the community, may be regular features in a local newspaper. Weather forecasts and times of sunrise and sunset might have been more important in farming communities, but also appeared in national newspapers.

Newspaper proprietors soon realised that many readers had a taste for the macabre, and by angling their reports accordingly could attract a greater readership and enhance their sales and profits. There were accounts of crimes and felonies, arson, burglaries, rapes, murders and suicides. Victims and criminals alike were described in great detail and often their innocent relations were included in the reports. If the supposed offenders were caught and apprehended, the names of those who assisted were usually published with the name of the constable making the arrest and the lock-up or gaol into which they were thrown. The accused may then have been taken to a court. In the past, as today, reports of court cases at assizes, quarter sessions, borough and petty sessions and coroners verdicts and sentences of magistrates and judges were regarded as 'good copy' and often worthy of extensive prose to the enormous benefit, even delight, of social and family historians. Some court cases, particularly highway robbery, sexual misbehaviour and murder, took up several columns in a local newspaper and were accompanied by sketches or photographs. A sentence imposing transportation to the colonies may provide further leads in tracing family members. If an execution was the final sentence, a second-by-second account of the events and the accused's last words was sometimes recorded. Disasters were reported with equal enthusiasm, shipwrecks and drownings, pit explosions, victims caught in factory machinery, children eaten by animals on Dartmoor, sweeps burned to death in chimneys, and whole households wiped out by malignant fevers or freak storms. Luckily for those of us using the newspapers today, many individuals, the victims of these disasters, and any heroes who attempted to save them, were named in the reports.

In many papers, increasingly through the 19th Century, there were advertisements for goods and services for sale, empty places on emigrant ships, and theatrical and musical concerts to attend. Many booksellers who also published newspapers, advertised their antiquarian bargains; a century earlier, James Read, Nathaniel Mist and Charles Baldwin, all booksellers, had each owned and published his own newspaper, although entitled 'Journals'. Rewards were offered if information led to the return of stolen goods, property, animals and people. Such features not only indicate the range of items on offer, but also their price and so enable you to understand better the lifestyle of your family. The unusually high number of advertisements for patent lotions and potions, all claiming to cure the strangest of ailments, is better understood when you discover the true full-time occupation of the newspaper's proprietor; in many cases he was a chemist or druggist, using his paper to advertise his wares and coincidently offer a local news service. The sales of shares in turnpike trusts or canal companies, and later of railway stock, were advertised from the late 18th Century.

Servants and apprentices sometimes ran away, or were occasionally kidnapped from their employers and masters; as a consequence advertisements with vivid descriptions of appearance, mannerisms and clothing were inserted into newspapers, offering a suitable recompense if they were returned safely. The person in the advertisement to whom a missing child was to be delivered was not always the father or the master; sometimes a brother or sister or other relation or friend was named, thereby providing you with further genealogical data. Possible places or persons to where or to whom the missing person may have gone are also suggested in some advertisements; which may offer you additional family relationships. There are also disturbing reports of wholesale kidnapping of children in London in the late 17th century and them being sold to the West Indies. Have you lost an ancestor's brother or sister around this time? Try looking in the *Flying Post* or the *Post Boy*, which published items such as these in their columns. Another reason for 'losing' family members could be that they changed their names. Such name changes, some by Royal licence, some by Act of Parliament, some by deed poll, others irregularly, were often advertised in the press. Most, but not all, by Royal assent were advertised in the *London Gazette* or *Dublin Gazette*, some others in *The Times*. A useful index to many changes of name advertised in papers from 1760 to 1901 was compiled and published in 1905 by W.P.W. Phillimore and E.A. Fry.

You can read of instances of bankruptcy or of a wife leaving her husband that he, through a newspaper notice, disclaimed all responsibility for debts she might be incurring. Occasionally a reward for her return was available. There were also advertisements for Wife Sales in the rural press, this being mistakenly thought to be a valid method of divorce, whereas the only valid way was by a Private Act of Parliament until 1857. Felons escaping from custody caused advertisements, appealing for information leading to their recapture, to be placed in both national and local papers and in the specialist periodical *Hue and Cry*, renamed the *Police Gazette* in 1828. Deserters from the armed forces were also described in this periodical as civilian police assistance was sought to apprehend and return the miscreants. Other advertisements for missing persons were from lawyers or relations attempting to locate them to advise them of a magnificent inheritance.

Periodicals have been known by a variety of terms: serial publications, journals, magazines even quarterlies and annuals if that was how often they were issued; but like newspapers many of them contain information which can be of value in historical research. If a newspaper was published less frequently than weekly, it tended to be called a periodical anyway; although when the Stamp Duty tax was imposed, the definition of a newspaper was a publication appearing more frequently than every 26 days. Some periodicals were associated with a trade or profession (the *Boot and Shoe Maker*, the *Pawnbrokers' Gazette*), or a religious denomination (the *Baptist Magazine*, the *British Friend*), or a hobby (*Family History News and Digest*); some were for families or of general interest (*Punch*, *Illustrated London News*), or particularly for historians (*Notes and Queries*, the *Reliquary*, the *Herald and Genealogist*). The founding dates of the above examples are given in the Selected List below. Although these were for specific interest groups, they were, and some still are, widely circulated and available on the open market by purchase or subscription. Other periodicals, such as school magazines and parish newsletters had a smaller circulation and in many instances carried more genealogical data.

Many professional periodicals contain not only complex and often highly technical articles on the minutiae of that profession, a new technique in the *Farrier and Naturalist*, or some exotic style in the *Hairdressers' Journal*; they also had reports on various meetings and news of members of their profession, promotions and transfers and in many cases notices of deaths and obituaries. The present-day journals of the scientific and engineering institutions are equally useful in providing personal biographies. School and college magazines and Old Boys' and Old Girls' Journals carry news on present and former staff and students, details on their careers and in some cases notes on marriages and births of children of former pupils. Some organisations produce Year Books with names and addresses of all their members which you may find extremely useful in your research. Parish and non-conformist newsletters may tell you names of organists, people on the flower rota, leaders of classes, as well as amounts collected for the restoration fund and occasionally short biographies of members of the congregation.

There are, of course, the normally annual publications of organisations such as the British Record Society, the Harleian Society, the Camden Society and a host of others, including county record and parish register societies; their main aims are to make considerably older manuscript material available to a wider readership (their subscribing members) by transcription, translation and publication. Whilst such regular publications may not be regarded as periodicals by everyone, they do contain vast amounts of genealogical data and should certainly be considered when undertaking historical research. Further information on these publications can be found in *Texts and Calendars* (see below under Indexes and in the Bibliography).

The Gentleman's Magazine was a unique monthly periodical, founded by Edward Cave in 1731 and continuing until 1907. For many years it was a compilation of news culled from the *London Gazette*, newspapers and other periodicals, and literary contributions (poetry, essays, book reviews and letters) received from various people. It made no secret of the majority of its sources of news and identified them on the first page of each issue. Cave, however, boosted his sales enormously by carrying accurate reports of parliamentary debates, astounding at the time as reporters were not permitted into the Commons, certainly not to make notes until 1803, as mentioned above.

It was later revealed that Cave smuggled a reporter, Guthrie, with a phenomenal memory into the House, who was later able to record near-enough verbatim reports of the proceedings. Until June 1868 the news items in the *Gentleman's Magazine* included reports of births, marriages and deaths, scientific discoveries, exceptional atmospheric conditions and multitudinous reports on the unusual and the bizarre, with numerous references to named individuals, ideal genealogical data. But from July 1868 to its demise in 1907, the *Gentleman's Magazine* concentrated almost exclusively on the literary contributions, and hence its use to family historians unfortunately dwindles. However, its use as a finding aid to its sources having further information is expanded on below, under Indexes.

THE WHEREABOUTS OF NEWSPAPERS AND PERIODICALS

To help locate specific newspapers or periodicals, it is useful to know what papers were printed anyway, both nationally and locally.

Family historians are most likely to be interested in local papers, and those of the past rather than the present. The F.F.H.S. has published a Guide to cater for these interests in *Local Newspapers, 1750–1920: England and Wales; Channel Islands; Isle of Man*, compiled by Jeremy Gibson (1987, updated to 1991). This is based upon thr British Library Newspaper Library catalogue mentioned below, but adds local library and record office holdings (but not those of newspaper offices themselves).

Over twenty local papers of the 1980s had origins before 1775. Several listings or 'Guides' or 'Directories' have been compiled annually which are really attempts by individuals, government agencies and commercial organisations, each to provide some sort of national inventory of current newspapers and periodicals. The best known of those which began in the 19th Century are those now published by Benn Brothers, beginning in 1846 as the *Newspaper Press Directory and Advertisers' Guide*, by Reed Information Services, beginning in 1873 as *Willing's Press Guide*, and by Sell, beginning in 1881 as *Sell's Directory of the World Press*. Both Benn's and Willing's concentrate on current newspapers and periodicals, although the latter has a section on immediately ceased publications, and have alphabetical and geographical listings. Years of origin and former titles are also given with addresses and telephone numbers of the current editorial offices. One or other of these publications is available in most public libraries and both are very easy to use. A useful gazetteer of English and Welsh newspapers, 1690 to 1981, arranged alphabetically under towns, was included in West's *Town Records* (see Bibliography), though for pre-1920 newspapers, this is effectively superseded by Gibson's *Local Newspapers.*

For periodicals, the *British Union Catalogue* lists all regular publications, apart from newspapers after 1799, held in British local collections and the Colindale collection from the 17th to the present centuries. This catalogue, held in large reference libraries, includes all periodicals published worldwide in British libraries but has the advantage of listing past publications, unlike Benn's and Willing's, although by searching back through their annual volumes some similar details could be found.

Copies of most British and Irish newspapers and periodicals, particularly from 1800, are held in the national collection at the British Library Newspaper Library, Colindale (address at the end of the Bibliography) which split from the British Museum in 1973. Their eight-volume catalogue was first published in 1975 and is available in other large libraries, although its very latest amendments are only at Colindale; the catalogue gives a complete list of holdings, although you will see that there are number of breaks in the runs of many titles. This catalogue is a major improvement to the 1920 *Tercentenary Handlist of English and Welsh Newspapers, Magazines and Reviews* published by the British Museum to record its inventory at that time. Unfortunately, when the Handlist was reproduced in 1966 it was a straight reprint and no attempt was made to update the list, which nearly 50 years later bore little relationship to the contemporary holdings. The Handlist should also be used with care as it represented the British Museum's holdings in 1920 and, in spite of what you may read in sales catalogues of book-dealers today advertising this book, is by no means a complete list of British newspapers and periodicals. Another disadvantage of the Handlist is that it is arranged chronologically and indexed by titles of publications, not places. The Newspaper Library Catalogue can be searched much more usefully by towns. Colindale is also organising 'Newsplan' in conjunction with local collections; this is a project to encourage the conservation and microfilming of newspapers throughout the country and to compile vast and comprehensive lists of holdings. Some pre-1800 British newspapers and very early newsbooks and news sheets are in the Burney Collection and the Thomason Tracts in the British (Museum) Library (in the Department of Printed Manuscripts), in the Bodleian Library at Oxford and in the University Library at Cambridge.

The British Library is publishing an important and definitive *Bibliography of British Newspapers*, though in almost twenty years only eight English counties, in six volumes, have yet been covered (see Bibliography).

The whereabouts of many Scottish newspapers held in various libraries in Scotland have been identified by Miss Fergusson in her *Directory of Scottish Newspapers* (see Bibliography). A very useful *Northern Ireland Newspapers; Checklist with Locations* has been produced jointly by the Library Association and the Public Record Office of Northern Ireland; this booklet lists alphabetically all the papers published from 1737 and identifies the whereabouts of collections having copies of the newspapers.

You may find that local newspaper collections in reference libraries and county record offices are more complete than at Colindale. In his *Town Records*, although published in 1983, John West asserts that there are many local collections of newspapers which are not recorded in the Newspaper Library Catalogue. Even local catalogues may not reveal what is actually held in a local library, so it is obviously worth your while asking around locally when trying to locate both national and local papers. The National Library of Wales has a comprehensive collection of newspapers published in Wales both in English and Welsh, whilst the National Libraries in Scotland and Dublin and the Belfast Public Library have equally comprehensive collections of Scottish and Irish newspapers. Trinity College Library in Dublin also has a fine collection of Irish newspapers. The Guildhall Library in London has a complete run of the *London Gazette* and most large reference libraries have complete sets of the *Gentleman's Magazine* from 1731. Many newspapers still engaged in active publication have copies of all their issues, although unfortunately most firms not have facilities where you can sit and read them.

INDEXES SPECIFICALLY TO NEWSPAPERS AND PERIODICALS

The publishers of newspapers provide indexes in only very exceptional circumstances. However, enthusiasts have prepared indexes of names and topics for certain newspapers; some of these indexes have been drawn exclusively from the births, marriages and deaths columns of a newspaper, some from only obituary notices, others from criminal court reports. Other indexes of names of individuals have used not only newspapers but other sources, and so it has been felt inappropriate to identify them here. Some examples of indexes specifically to newspaper items are:

Dorset	a Newspaper Index, held by Mrs. D. Giles.
Kent	lists of entries in the *Kentish Gazette* 1787–89, held by Mr. D. Harrington.
London	the Andrews Index of notices taken mostly from the *London Gazette*, held by the Institute of Heraldic and Genealogical Studies.
Norfolk/Suffolk	indexes of Births, Marriages and Deaths in the *Bury and Norfolk Post* 1794–1830, held at Colindale.
Staffordshire	*Staffordshire Advertiser: Index to Births, Marriages and Deaths 1795–1820*, published by the Staffordshire Record Society in 1968.
Warwickshire	an Index to Births, Marriages and Deaths from the *Warwick Advertiser* 1806–32, held by Mrs. P. Page.
Jersey	an Index from Jersey Newspapers 1870–1905 held at the Societé Jersiaise.

Further details on these, such as search fees and addresses of the holders, are given in Gibson and Hampson's *Marriage, Census and other Indexes for Family Historians* or in Gibson's *Local Newspapers 1750–1920* (see Bibliography).

The *Index to The Times* in quarterly volumes from 1 October 1790 to 30 June 1941, begun by C.J. Palmer in the 19th Century, and now produced annually by the publishers as the *Official Index to the Times* (which actually began in 1907), is one which is often quoted as being typical of use to genealogists; but it is not typical and is useful only for certain items. The period from 1 January 1785, when the *Daily Universal Register* (the former name for *The Times*) was established, to 1790 has also been officially indexed in recent years. Almost all entries, however, are from the upper strata of society, and after 1837 Palmer omitted all births, marriages and deaths as he felt that civil registration from that date obviated the need for him to include them. Palmer's extensive work has few references to 'ordinary' people and his arrangement of names was under topics, rather than a complete alphabetical listing. Nevertheless, it is extremely useful if you are looking for someone from the higher walks of life, and he did include references to wills having been proved and the values of the estates. The *Official Indexes* are easier to use as they do have complete alphabetical listings but, of course, go back only to 1907 in the later series. A separate *Official Index to*

Obituaries in The Times from 1951—75 has also been produced by the publishers.

Ashton's *Old Times* on social life at the end of the 18th century was compiled in 1885 exclusively from reports in *The Times*. As this work is divided into categories and is extremely well indexed, it effectively acts as an index to selected items for 1788—99 taken from *The Times*. His *Dawn of the 19th Century*, taken mostly from contemporary newspapers, and also well-indexed is less easy to use in locating the items in the original papers; it is, nevertheless, fascinating reading.

The publishers of very many periodicals produced indexes on a yearly or five-yearly or other conveniently frequent basis. In general, periodical indexes are far more comprehensive and hence, more useful than the older indexes to newspapers. The former were normally issued in a similar format to the periodical so that a number of issues could be bound with the index into volumes for better keeping and reference. Indexes for some periodicals have been prepared by enthusiastic amateurs and by record office staffs in their spare time. Some of the older indexes are on card or in manuscript, such as that held in the Naval Historical Library to naval obituaries from the *Naval and Military Gazette*. For technical periodicals there was rarely a comprehensive index to all persons named in the text of every issue, although authors and editors of articles were usually well indexed as were the topics covered in the periodicals. A useful way to locate articles in periodicals published by the older record societies, county historical societies, historical associations and similar groups is through some publications of the Royal Historical Society: Mullins' two volumes of *Texts and Calendars* and the Stevensons' *Scottish Texts and Calendars* (see Bibliography), which are themselves indexed, list under the periodical for each society a volume-by-volume account of the titles and a very brief precis of the articles in each volume.

As mentioned above, the periodical *Gentleman's Magazine* (GM) was put together monthly very much by abstracting items from other publications. Every six months a preface and indexes were printed so that subscribers could have their magazines bound into half-yearly indexed volumes. The indexes were organised by literary topics and by surnames. As an additional finding aid, cumulative indexes were produced for all volumes to 1786 and from 1786 to 1819; and in 1922 E.A. Fry produced an index to the marriages that had appeared in the GM from 1731 to 1768. An even more comprehensive index was prepared by the Church of Jesus Christ of Latter Day Saints (the LDS

Church or Mormons) from a slip index held at the College of Arms. As the GM is effectively a compendium or precis of major reports from other periodicals and newspapers, it is, in itself, a finding aid and a way into those publications. You can, accordingly, look initially in one of the GM's cumulative or half-yearly indexes to locate an entry; then read the account of the event in the appropriate volume to discover the date on which it took place. You can then turn to a national or local newspaper or periodical of around that date, where you will most likely find a fuller account of the event, or a more comprehensive article about an individual, perhaps one of your ancestors.

Genealogical periodicals vary greatly in the quality of their indexes regarding names of individuals; in many cases every individual named within an article is not indexed. Most of the genealogical periodicals which began in the 19th century (see the Selected List below) were indexed. However, since 1991 some of these have been totally re-indexed by Stuart Raymond under authors, family names and places. He has also re-grouped the titles of all the articles in order of counties under topics. Raymond's extensive work has been published by the F.F.H.S. as a series of bibliographies of the contents of *British Genealogical Periodicals* (see Bibliography).

The Digest central section of *Family History News and Digest* (see Selected List of Periodicals) is more than a cumulative index to all articles relating to genealogy, heraldry and family history which have appeared in a very wide range of periodicals since 1977. Each article has been condensed to a two- or three-line description (an abstract) of its contents and those abstracts have been indexed under suitable headings of topic and location by country and county or region. Each abstract gives the title of the article, the author's name, the title, volume and part number and date of the periodical in which the article first appeared, enabling you to refer back readily to the original.

Alphabetical indexes to names from obituaries in many newspapers and periodicals, including some published in America, were published as annual volumes for 1880, 1881 and 1882 by the British Record Society, edited by H.B. Wheatley. One- or two-line biographies of the deceased are included in these annual indexes, available in some reference libraries. The British Record Society in 1891 also published an *Index to Biographical and Obituary Notices from 1731—1780*, edited by E.A. Fry.

Musgrave's *Obituary*, a compilation rather than an index, was prepared by abstracting obituary notices relating to England,

Scotland and Ireland, mainly from periodicals such as the *London Magazine*, *Gentleman's Magazine*, *Scots Magazine* and the *European Magazine* up to 1800, but not from newspapers. Its contents can be judged from the sources used by Sir William Musgrave. The results of his labours were published by the Harleian Society from 1899 to 1901 in their volumes 44—49.

There is a record at Colindale of all newspaper indexes of which the authorities there are aware, but it is known that other newspaper indexes do exist for local and national newspapers compiled by individuals and organisations but not advertised widely. Newspaper indexes that were drawn to the attention of the contributors of the *National Index of Parish Registers* (NIPR), published by the Society of Genealogists, have been included in those volumes, although the completeness and quality of the indexes in general are not identified. In general, the NIPR newspaper indexes are not included in the booklet by Gibson and Hampson, although some appear in Gibson's *Local Newspapers*.

Irish newspapers have been particularly well indexed by Rosemary ffolliott, who has written several articles on her work in numerous books on Irish genealogical research.

A SELECTED LIST OF PERIODICALS

Listed below are some periodicals and magazines from the 18th century, which may be of particular interest to family and social historians. Some were for a specialist readership, others have articles and illustrations that today's historians will find useful when gathering background or specific information to accompany their own material. Although most were intended to be regular publications when first issued, some were spasmodically produced and some were short-lived. Quarterly Journals of the Member Societies of the Federation of Family History Societies have not been included; these can be found in Perkins' *Current Publications by Member Societies* (see Bibliography), whilst abstracts of their articles, suitably indexed, can be found in *Family History News and Digest*, as explain above.

Copies of all the following periodicals are held in the British Library at Colindale: details of access, opening hours, etc. are given at the end of the Bibliography. The year indicates the date when the periodical was first published. Local and national newspapers are not included; for a county-by-county listing of local papers see J.S.W. Gibson's book and for all newspapers and periodicals see the

Colindale Library Catalogue, details of which are in the Bibliography.

1717 *Historical Register* (covered events from 1714).
1731 *Gentleman's Magazine*.
1758 *Annual Register*.
1793 *Evangelical Magazine* (Congregationalists).
1793 *Bulletins of the Campaign* (to 1815).
1798 *Methodist Magazine* (continued as *Wesleyan Methodist Magazine* to 1932).
1799 *Naval Chronicle* (to 1818).
1802 *General Baptist Registry* (General Baptists).
1802 *Cobbett's Annual/Weekly/Political Register*.
1807 *Antiquary's Magazine*.
1809 *Baptist Magazine* (Particular Baptists).
1810 *Account of the Times and Places of holding the Meetings for Worship and the Quarterly Meetings of the Society of Friends in Great Britain* (to 1888).
1816 *Orthodox Journal and Catholic Monthly Intelligencer*.
1819 *Primitive Methodist Magazine* (to 1932).
1824 *National School Magazine*.
1828 *Hue and Cry* (later the *Police Gazette* and from 1835 the *People's Police Gazette*).
1828 *Farrier and Naturalist* (continued as *Hippiatrist and Veterinary Journal*).
1829 *Canal Boatman's Magazine*.
1833 *Naval and Military Gazette* (to 1886).
1834 *Collectanea Topographica et Genealogica* (edited by J.G. Nicholls).
1836 *Symons' Meteorological Magazine*.
1837 *Justice of the Peace*.
1838 *Pawnbrokers' Gazette*.
1841 *Punch*.
1842 *Illustrated London News*.
1843 *British Friend* (Quakers, to 1913).
1843 *Chapman's Weekly Magazine*.
1846 *Bakers' Union* (continued as *Master Bakers' and Confectioners Society*; continued as *Bakers' Times*).
1846 *Topographer and Genealogist: a New Series of Collectanea Topographica et Genealogica* (to 1858).
1847 *Mechanic's Organ: A Journal for Young Men and Women*.
1849 *New Wonderful Magazine: A Collection of Remarkable Trials, Biographies, etc.*

1849 *Notes and Queries*.
1852 *Lifeboat* or *Journal of the National Shipwreck Institution*.
1853 *General Weekly Shipping List*.
1853 *Moravian Magazine*.
1856 *Missing Friends and Australian Advertiser*.
1856 *Masonic Observer*.
1857 *Poor Law Unions' Gazette*.
1860 *Reliquary*.
1861 *Fun* (incorporated with *Sketchy Bits* in 1893).
1862 *Grocer*.
1863 *Hairdresser's Journal*.
1863 *Herald and Genealogist* (edited by J.G. Nichols).
1864 *Archers' Register*.
1865 *Landed Families of Great Britain: a Quarterly Journal of Genealogical Research* (edited by J.C. Whimper).
1866 *Licensed Victuallers' Gazette*.
1866 *Miscellanea Genealogica et Heraldica* (edited by J.J. Howard).
1866 *Tailor and Cutter*.
1877 *Genealogist* (edited by G.W. Marshall).
1878 *Boot and Shoe Maker* (continued as *Boot and Shoe Trades Journal*).
1888 *Butcher*.
1894 *Farriers' Journal*.
1895 *Greengrocer, Fruiterer and Market Gardener* (continued as *Fruitgrower*).
1896 *Genealogical Queries and Memoranda* (edited by G.F.T. Sherwood).
1896 *Matrimonial Intelligencer*.
1906 *Ancestor: a Quarterly Review of County and Family History, Heraldry and Antiquities*.
1913 *Genealogical Monthly*.
1925 *Genealogists' Magazine* (Society of Genealogists).
1952 *Amateur Historian* (continued in 1968 as *Local Historian*).
1962 *Family History* (Institute of Heraldic and Genealogical Studies).
1977 *Family History News and Digest* (Federation of Family History Societies).
1981 *Irish Links*.
1984 *Family Tree Magazine*.

BIBLIOGRAPHY

Local Newspapers 1750—1920, J.S.W. Gibson, F.F.H.S., 1987 (updated 1991).

A Directory of Scottish Newspapers, J.P.S. Fergusson, National Library of Scotland, 1984.

The English Newspaper, Stanley Morrison, Cambridge University Press, 1932.

Dangerous Estate, Francis Williams, Longmans, 1957.

Town Records, J. West, Phillimore, 1983.

Old Times, J. Ashton, Nimmo, 1885.

Dawn of the 19th Century in England, J. Ashton, 1890.

News from the English Countryside, C. Morsley, Harrap, 1979.

British Newspapers, Brian Lake, Sheppard Press, 1984.

Freshest Advices, R.M. Wiles, Ohio State University Press, 1965.

The Beginnings of the English Newspaper 1620—1660, Joseph Frank, Harvard University Press, 1961.

The Development of the Provincial Newspaper 1700—1760, G.A. Cranfield, 1962.

Studies in the Early English Periodical, Richmond P. Bond, University of North Carolina Press, 1957.

The Newspaper Press in Britain, D. Linton and R. Boston, Massell, 1987.

Origins of the Popular Press 1855—1914, A.J. Lee, Croom Helm, 1976.

A Census of British Newspapers and Periodicals 1620—1800, R.S. Craze and F.B. Kaye, 1927; republished by Holland Press, 1966.

British Newspapers and Periodicals 1641—1700, C. Nelson and M. Seccombe, Modern Language Association of America, 1977.

British Literary Magazines 1698—1788, A. Sullivan, Greenwood Press. 1983.

Index and Finding List of Serials Published in the British Isles, W. Seward, University of Kentucky Press, 1953.

Wellesley Index to Victorian Periodicals 1824—1900, Vols. 1—5, W.E. Houghton, 1966; reprinted by Routledge, 1988.

Texts and Calendars (of English and Welsh serial publications to 1956), E.L.C. Mullins, Royal Historical Society, 1958, reprinted 1978.

Texts and Calendars II (1957—82), E.L.C. Mullins, Royal Historical Society, 1983.

Scottish Texts and Calendars, D. and W.B. Stevenson, Royal Historical Society, 1987.

The Advertisers' Aid, The Newspaper Society (a regular publication from the 1940s).

Newspaper Press Directory and Advertisers Guide, C. Mitchell, Benn Bros. (a regular, often annual, publication from 1846).
Sell's Directory of the World Press, H. Sell (a regular publication from 1881).
Willing's Press Guide, Reed Information Services (an annual publication from 1873 by a succession of publishers).
Bibliography of British Newspapers, The British Library (a series covering counties; so far published are: Wiltshire, 1975; Durham and Northumberland, 1982, Kent, 1982; Derbyshire, 1987; Nottinghamshire, 1987; Cornwall and Devon, 1991).
Journal of Newspaper and Periodical History, Meckler Corporation (a regular publication from 1984).
Marriage, Census, and other Indexes for Family Historians, J.S.W. Gibson and E. Hampson, Federation of Family History Societies, 1992.
Current Publications by Member Societies, J.P. Perkins, Federation of Family History Societies, 1992.
Catalogue of English Newspapers and Periodicals in the Bodleian Library 1622–1820, R.T. Mitford and D.M. Sutherland, Bodleian Library, 1936.
Catalogue of the Newspaper Library, Colindale, Vols. 1–8, British Museum Publications, 1975.

The Newspaper Library is located in Colindale Avenue, London NW9 5HE. (Tel: 081-2005515). Colindale Underground Station (Northern Line) is across the road. Parking nearby. Open Monday to Saturday 10 a.m. to 5 p.m. Write or telephone in advance for details on procuring a reader's ticket. There is a refreshment room on the premises.

OTHER USEFUL ADDRESSES

Federation of Family History Societies, The Benson Room, Birmingham and Midland Institute, Margaret Street, Birmingham B3 3BS.
National Library of Wales, Aberystwyth, Dyfed SY23 3BU (Tel: 0970-3816).
National Library of Scotland, George IV Bridge, Edinburgh EH1 1EW (Tel: 031-226-4531).
Belfast Public Library, Royal Avenue, Belfast BT1 1EA (Tel: 0232-243233).
National Library of Ireland, Kildare Street, Dublin 2 (Tel: 010-353-1-765521).

Trinity College, College Street, Dublin 2 (Tel: 010-353-1-772941).
Guildhall Library, Aldermanbury, London EC2P 2EJ (Tel: 071-260-1863).
University Library, West Street, Cambridge CB3 9DR (Tel: 0223-333143).
Bodleian Library, Oxford OX1 3BG. (Tel: 0865-277000).
Society of Genealogists, 14 Charterhouse Buildings, Goswell Road, London EC1M 7BA.
Scottish Genealogy Society, 15 Victoria Terrace, Edinburgh EH1 2JL.
Institute of Heraldic and Genealogical Studies, Northgate, Canterbury, Kent CT1 1BA.
Family Tree Magazine, 61 Great Whyte, Ramsey, Huntingdon PE17 1HL.